Odd as F*c

Anne Walsh Donnelly

First published May 2021 by Fly on the Wall Press

Published in the UK by Fly on the Wall Press

56 High Lea Rd, New Mills, Derbyshire, SK22 3DP

www.flyonthewallpress.co.uk

Copyright Anne Walsh Donnelly © 2021

ISBN: 9781913211424 Paperback

9781913211431 EBook

The right of Anne Walsh Donnelly to be identified as the author of this work has been asserted in accordance with the Copyright, Designs and Patents Act 1988. Typesetting by Isabelle Kenyon. Cover photo from Shutterstock.

This collection is dedicated to mothers who have lost children and children who have lost mothers, especially those I've been privileged to spend time with on this earth.

Acknowledgments

Thanks to the Words Ireland Mentorship Programme 2020, the Mayo Arts Office and my mentor Nuala O'Connor for their support. To Fly on the Wall press, in particular Isabelle Kenyon for her editorial input, enthusiasm and for being such a pleasure to work with.

Thanks to the Poetry Ireland Introduction Series 2019 which contributed to my development as a poet. To Martina Evans for selecting me for the series and my fellow poets who participated in the series.

Thanks to the editors and journals where some of the poems (or earlier versions) in this collection first appeared: *Crannog, Boyne Berries, The Blue Nib, Impspired, Impossible Archetype, Poetry Bus, Inside the Bell Jar, Live Encounters, Havin' A Laugh, Poethead* and *Spontaneity*.

Thanks to the many poets and writers I have been fortunate to encounter since I started writing. You are too many to mention, but in particular I'd like to acknowledge the following groups: *Museum Writers Group, Poets Abroad, Crows Foot Group, GMIT Creative Writing Class of 2013, Over the Edge Online Writing Workshops* and most especially my *Weekly Prompts Writing Group*.

Deep gratitude and much love as always goes to my parents, brothers and two children, Brian and Hannah.

Contents

May I show you
the crumpled autumn leaf
on the pavement?
Will you walk with me
towards the first bud of spring?

Days Like These

I

I kneel beside my bed, in my pink-striped nightie
look out the window at the sky and say, *Hi.*

God sits on a gold throne on the biggest cloud,
scratching his white beard, smiling
like my brother's Action Man doll.
Mam told me today her Mother died
when she was fourteen.

I wonder if she's with God.
I blow my mousey-brown fringe out of my eyes
and promise Him I'll do anything as long
as he doesn't take my Mam.

I'll go to Mass every day,
say my prayers every night.
I'll always love Him the most,
then Mam, Dad, my brothers
and everyone else in the whole universe.
I'll never put myself first.

II

I slam shut my New Jerusalem Bible.
Where the hell has He gone?

One of His priests announced today in scripture
class that there was never a stable or donkeys
or angels in the sky or shepherds or wise men.
If that's a myth, what's the truth?

I graduate with an honours degree,
my head full of God's knowledge,
my heart empty.

III

I leave Ireland to find what I'm looking for,
even though I don't know what that is.

I trek through ice and snow in the Canadian Rockies,
stand on the edge of the Grand Canyon, stare into the abyss,
climb red rock at Uluru.
I'm in awe of these natural works of beauty
but feel no sense of my God.

I spend a week in Ubud and grow jealous
of the Balinese people's devotion to their Gods.
Every morning I open the door of my room
and on the step sits a small palm leaf full of white,
red, yellow, and blue petals.
Floral notes and incense touch my nose.

'*Canang sari*', says the woman of the house,
'*to offer thanks to Sang Hyang Widhi Wasa*'.

Everywhere I walk I see offerings,
outside shops, cafes, beside fishing boats on the beach.
I don't know or understand the Balinese Hindu Gods
but they reside in old men's faces, laughing monkeys,
and temple echoes. The Balinese eat, sleep, work,
and dance with their Gods. I leave the island,
grieving for the loss of my faith: yearning to find my God again.

IV

I promise I will love and honour this man until death.
I experience the miracle of creation
when I give birth. My children are baptised.
I help them draw pictures of the Holy Man in the sky,
and bring them to Mass, every Sunday.

I stop when I break my vows and leave my marriage.
For the first time in my life, I have put myself first

and flagellate myself daily for doing so.
I fall in love with a woman,
consummate the relationship
and am now considered to be 'intrinsically disordered.'
I ex-communicate myself.
Even if I could find my God,
I am not worthy of His love.

V

I stand in the shadow of a lone oak tree,
on the edge of a November river,
and stare into its bog-brown waters.
I have given up hoping before I go to sleep,
that I won't wake the next morning.
I wish I could pierce my body and bleed out the depression,
that eats my insides, cramps my stomach,
and smothers my will to live.

The wind howls, crows caw, a bull roars in a distant field.
Even now, as I stand on the edge of my death,
God stays silent. Instead, the words my daughter said
yesterday come to my mind,

'Mam, please don't die before me.'

I drag my hands through cropped crimson hair.
Love casts a net around my body.
I can't even kill myself, I think,
struggling to escape the net's scratchy rope.
The wind steals tears from my eyes. God stays silent.

I visit my therapist. On her table lie three angel cards,

Divine Timing, Answered Prayer, Divine Guidance

'I drew them for you,' she says.

I wonder if God is touching me

through others. I hope He is.

VI

A childhood prayer, I used to chant at Benediction,
pops into my head as I drive to work:

O Sacrament most holy
O Sacrament Divine
All praise and all thanksgiving
Be every moment thine.

It resonates as I drive home from work,
cook dinner, kiss my children goodnight, brush my teeth,
hop into bed and close my eyes. This prayer surfaces
again and again, as inexplicable
as a raisin rising from the bottom of an under-baked cake.

I dream of entering a cellar, illuminated by a single candle.
A veiled being sits on a stool, I whisper,

'You've come back to me?'
'I never left.'

Who are you? Mother? Father?
What pronoun do I use? He, She, They?
What do I call you? Universe, Source, Divine?

I separate letters, shuffle them around the Scrabble board
of my being, try to find what fits,
throw them into the air, watch them land.
There's no word to describe what I've found – within me.

The glacier of disbelief begins to melt.
I sit in silence, my muscles relax
and I feel a hand, not of this earth, on my shoulder.
I close my eyes, press the pause button
on unanswered questions, rest in the mystery.

In the space between the end of one breath
and the beginning of another, I feel a quiver
run through me, that could possibly be divinity.

I still can't say for certain if I've found
what I've yearned for.
But maybe, just maybe, God is,

My   Greatness.
My   Ordinariness.
In   Days like these.

II

Conversations

I hope when you leave
I will sit at the kitchen table
sip strong tea from your china cup
and recall a conversation
where you might have said,
'I love you.'

I hope I'll forget the evening
I sat beside you on the couch
turned my face to you expectantly
as you watched the nine-o-clock news.
You yawned, leaned away and said,
'You're getting too old for goodnight kisses.'

I hope when I finish my tea
and go from the kitchen
into the front room and lean
over the body you've outgrown,
I'll be able to let myself say,
'I love you, Mammy.'

Soon

Remember the day your mother
left you in the isolation ward,
said she'd be back *soon*.
Soon was the length of time,
it took to eat a pack of *Jelly Tots*.

When it took longer than *soon*
for her to return
you vacuum-packed your heart
promised never to unwrap it,
expose yourself to germs again.

1957 - 1959

On the hottest Sunday in July,
the same day Mam got her first period,
she was sent to her father's room
to wake him for tea.

She cried when she touched his tepid skin
and begged him to open his eyes.
In the fields cattle lowed, udders heavy with milk.

Two Christmases later,
my grandmother pressed Mam's hand
against her abdomen,
told her of the operation in January.
'I'm afraid I might not wake up.'

'You mustn't cry,
you have to be strong for your sisters,'
the nuns told Mam, the day before the funeral.

She watched over her sisters
as they stood shivering in the graveyard,
under the shadow of a Great Oak.
She became the roots of their saplings,
chainsawed through her own pain.

Branded

A violet amoeba stain marked my cheek.
Mam told me it was a crocus,
the doctor said it was benign.

Every day it spread through my body
like black spot on a rose leaf.
Each anniversary of her mother's death
lesions erupted, burned the skin

on the underside of my wrists.
When I was dragged into the dark alleyways
of teenage-hood, she told me I was too old

for hugs. A coffin encased her heart.
I could no longer hear its beat.
Incense from her mother's funeral
tainted the tip of her tongue.

Just as she once did, I tied
a mother's apron
around a thirteen-year-old waist.

A Minute's Silence

Your tightly
closed eyelids
hid bog holes.

Your gentle face
creased with trenches
of grief.

Your vulnerability
roared in a minute's silence.
I shivered.

Your frailty hurtled
into my heart and stayed
surrounded by fierce love.

Life resumed,
but differently.

Klein's Breast

She had the breast of a cow goddess,
that imparted the strength of a pharaoh.

The ducts were blocked, milk dammed,
to create a reservoir, for the next baby.

At university I wondered if she had
Melanie Klein's bad or good breast, or both.

In her hospital bed, they clung to her sternum,
shriveled, redundant, like two burst balloons.

The left plate of her face dented by a stroke.
The right, half of her wedding day smile.

I pretended to understand her words,
as I wiped dribble from her chin.

The Apple Tart

She sliced bruised Brambleys
laid them in circles on the pastry
sprinkled with sugar and cloves
covered with more pastry
forked the lid with holes
to release hot air,
then brushed with egg.

I watched her pick flour
from crevices in calloused hands.
A *whoosh* of hot air filled the kitchen
when she opened the oven's door
and slid the tart inside.

I filled the kettle
anticipating crumbling pastry on lips
cloved apple on tongues
and the strong tea we'd drink
before the men came home.

Conkers

I stand under the canopy of a Horse Chestnut tree,
wait for a conker as strong as Cúchulainn to drop.
The mist dampening my face turns torrential,
a breeze bolts through the branches like a train.

I split the thorny, green shell that lands
on the toe of my shoe,
inspect the conker, roll it between my palms.
I feel like a warrior ready for battle.

Mrs Brennan nurses a mug of lukewarm tea in the kitchen,
and tells Mam about the trollop
that has gone and got herself pregnant.

I get Dad's screwdriver,
bore a hole in my conker.
It gets stuck halfway through.

'She'll have to leave school now,' says Mrs Brennan,
in a voice that reminds me of the Joker in *Batman*.

'The buck that did it won't have to,' says Mam.

The table trembles as I bang the conker
and force the screwdriver out the arse end.
It smashes into pieces.

A lump lands in Mrs Brennan's mug.
Mam scoops the remains into her hands and says,
'Go play with your dolls, like a good girl.'

Mother's Day, 2020

I won't walk in your front door, say *hello,* sit by the stove
listen to timber crackle and simply be with you.

I remember the last cup of tea and dinner you prepared for me.
I remember the last time I hugged the bones of you,
felt your warmth, saw the look of love in your eyes.

I don't know when I can be with you again. Weeks? Months?
Our phone calls have become even more precious.

All I want to do is drive home, stand on the front lawn,
look through the kitchen window, watch you smile and wave.

All I can do is go into my own garden, release the love
in my heart, watch it float towards the clouds and hope
some divine creature will bring it home to you.

Today is a Mother's Day like no other.

You Tell Me

I have to say goodbye
to your hearth, amber turf
and smoke that soothes like incense.

Goodbye to the dust lounging
on windowsills
and the upturned corner
of your threadbare mat.

Goodbye to the dolls
asleep on your shelf,
Winnie the Pooh tea cups
and tannin stains.

Goodbye to your velvet scarf
on my ice cream neck
and *Imperial Leather* scent
orbiting our armchairs.

Goodbye to our laughter
detonating bath bombs on skin
and silences filled
with whispering ash leaves.

Goodbye to your crying lines,
swollen wrists and ankles,
your crutch leaning against the mantel,
the shine in your pupils.

I stand and ask,
'Can I bring your burnt-orange
cushion home with me?'

III

I'm a Jack Hammer

in his builder hands. Days
I lie on the floor of his *Hiace* van,
marinating in diesel fumes,
bent nails for company.

I come to life when he grabs my neck
plugs me into the power socket
stands me on a slab of concrete,
his feet positioned either side of my body.

He tilts me back towards his bullish-hulk,
presses my chiselled tip
into a crack on the pavement
and squeezes my trigger.

I machine-gun into life,
frightening children at play,
and myself, with the noise I make.
Foam plugs in his ears,

gripper gloves on his hands,
safety glasses over his eyes,
while my naked head
hammers into cement and stone.

Powerless to stop, I demolish the path
that lies before me. Chunks of concrete
fly through the air like crazed Spitfires
until he takes his finger off the trigger.

When finished, he wipes chalk-grey
dust from his hi-vis vest, throws me
back into his rusting *Hiace* van.
I wait until he grabs me again.

The Knife Thrower's Wife

Sylvester & Barbara Baum were a professional knife throwing act.

Trust sharpens her husband's blades
before each act. She lets him strap
her to a plank of wood
buckled by wrist and ankle.

Knowing that she'll survive
his onslaught, she tells him,
to do what he has to do,
no matter how bloody that might be.

He holds each knife by its steel blade
and with a flick of his wrist
lets it fly in a half-spin towards her,
(with much less skill than Sylvester Baum).

Trust doesn't flinch when a knife lands
millimeters from the tip of her right ear
or another grazes her left thumbnail.
'More,' she says,

until there's nothing left to throw.
After the applause, she pulls each knife
from the plank, locks them in their steel case
until they are needed again.

Birth to Bacon

Life is
fighting with other piglets
to latch onto mother's teat,
getting too close to her belly,
and risking suffocation.

Life is
rolling in a mucky sty,
gorging on mulched turnips.

Life is
delivering your own brood,
killing half, unbeknownst
to yourself as you labour.

Life is
running around the farmyard,
through squawking hens
and strutting cocks
to escape the butcher's knife.

And you wonder
what you could have done
differently.

Simmering Orange Sauce

Hope is mouse peeking out of his hole
one eye on a sliver of grated cheese
lying on the kitchen floor
the other on the sleeping Labrador
near the patio door.

Hope is woman hunched over the oven hob
watching two duck breasts
blacken on the frying pan
stirring a simmering orange sauce
hearing the tick of the kitchen clock.

Hope is man, gulping *one last pint*
as the barman calls closing time
car keys lodged in his jeans pocket
he plans the drive home
via the bog road.

Hope is dog, raising an eyelid
he listens for the patter of tiny feet
dreams of sinking his teeth into mouse meat
or perhaps a breast drizzled with orange sauce
that he'll find in the green bin.

Rare Rib-Eye

If I hadn't turned the key in the ignition
like you ordered me to before we married,
we wouldn't be where we are now.
I'd never have learned to drive
never have sat outside the bank,
engine running, waiting

for you to finish work.
I'd never have seen you get into her
yellow Toyota Yaris.
I'd have been at home, reading your text,
have to stay late don't wait up
while watching Corrie.

I'd never have seen her yellow shoe box
bounce up and down in the carpark.
She, riding you as if you were a stallion.
I'd never have smashed that Yaris's grin,
head on. No, I'd have been in the kitchen,
stirring a blue-cheese sauce
to pour over your rare rib-eye steak.

Venus

Was there ever a more heavenly time
than the day I found you, naked
in a Botticelli print, perfect curves,
thigh-length hair covering your core?

From semen of the gonads of Kronos,
you stood on a giant scallop shell,
ready to alight on a Cyprus beach.
Baby Goddess, Aura blew your golden strands

towards me, brushed my flushed cheeks.
Your salt drops landed on the tip of my nose,
your peppermint and eucalyptus breath
cleared my mucus.

I lost you, standing in front of another Botticelli,
you lay in a grove of myrtle
shrouded in a vintage white gown.
I watched you watch Mars sleep

as wasps hovered around his head
and infant satyrs played with his lance.
Then I returned home to Vulcan,
his blacksmith hammer and forge heat.

Odd as F*ck

Bridie, did I tell you, Victoria dyed her hair,
same colour as a hawthorn berry?
I nearly choked on the Body of Christ
when she knelt beside me at the altar on Sunday.

I knew the day herself and Jim
got married it wouldn't last.

Dancing like a goat up the aisle, no Father
to give her away, no proper hymns at the Mass,
just some of that Chris De Burgh shite
all the young wans are into nowadays.

Wearing a purple velvet dress,
and rainbow earrings. Her five brothers
were the bridesmaids. As himself said,
'Odd as f*ck.'

I told Jim, she didn't save herself for him.
And do you know what he said to me?
'Ma, the only virgins in this town are the nuns.'

Paid no heed to my warnings.
I know sons never do. Think us mammies are eejits.
Not an eejit now he's back in his own bedroom,
waking up to the smell of a fry every day.

She wasn't domesticated either. I could smell
the steak burning from our house. Every sponge cake
she made in that fancy new range collapsed.

Poor Jim was like an orphan lamb with no ewe
to feed him. We're all as well off without her.
God only knows what kind of kids she'd have produced.

And she wouldn't be the type of woman
that'd mind himself and myself in our old age.

Wasn't it awful sad about Dick Hanley?
Only 69. Maggie will find it hard to manage the farm
on her own. I hear her daughter's moving home
from Dublin, got a teaching job in Ballina.

She'll be on the hunt for a man.
A laying hen like her will have no bother getting one.

Bridie, did I tell you?
Jim's applied for an annulment.
I'm posting his application now.

The Death of Happy-ever-afters

After Ruth Ellen Kocher

The time of happy-ever-after's
ended the day
my father told me
of my cousin James' death.
The same day
a text on my husband's phone
murdered our marriage.
Later,
I read my daughter
nursery rhymes, imagining
James' body
falling to the ground,
the thud against dried earth,
the squawk of crows lifted
from branches
of nearby Ash trees,
by the crack
of a shotgun.
Not once, but twice.

After the funeral,
I watched my daughter
take her first steps
in my mother's kitchen.
We clapped her efforts,
I resisted the urge
to put out my hand
when she wobbled,
knowing
I could no longer
deny the reality
that sometimes
mothers have to bury
their own children
and wives have to leave
their husbands.

The Wonder of You

In St Stephen's Green
Park, two women
watch children
throw stale crusts
to hungry ducks.

They listen to Dickie Rock
sing, *The wonder of you*
from an old man's
transistor radio.

They stroke
their newly-styled
beehive hair,
sit side by side,
feel a heat stronger
than August sun.

They dare to lick
each other's cone,
wary of eyes
that might stone dead
their intrinsically
disordered love.

The Ploughed Field

After The Fall of Icarus by Pieter Bruegel

In the painting hanging on her bedroom wall,
a castle rises from sea, colour of teal.
Two ships circle the ruin.
On a cliff stands a boy, tending a flock of sheep.
He watches a horse pull a plough,
its handles an extension of his father's arms.
The iron blades dig furrows into black soil.

I rise from underneath her turquoise duvet.
Her two Cocker Spaniels circle the bed.
On the window ledge stands a photo of a boy,
one hand held by her, the other by his father.
He stares at me.
I turn my back to him, pull the duvet
over her bare shoulders, stroke the ridges
her marriage has shaped in her forehead
and hope my skin will fill the space within.

IV

To Be a Stranger in Your Own Home

After John Clare

You go home for Mam's brown soda bread,
and her apple tart pastry crumbling in your mouth.

You go home to thaw your frozen heart beside the fire,
listen to your Dad's corny jokes.

The burning coal blasts heat, measles your cheeks.
Your Mam's eyes flit over you, her mouth opens,

'You've lost weight, you're very pale,
You mustn't be looking after yourself.'

You squirm in the armchair, leather creaks.
Your Dad, eyes on his newspaper, waits.

You can't remember the child picking wild strawberries
in the silver framed photo on the mantelpiece.

You yawn goodnight and don't let your bituminous thoughts
contaminate the space between.

Muffled words encased in watery tones float from your
parents' bedroom, twenty thousand leagues above you.

An oil slick mats the feathers of pelicans and penguins
dotted on the duvet covering your sweaty body.

A snare clenches the paw of your nightmares.
You leave before they wake.

You must be the consumer of your own woes,
take them wherever you go.

October, 2016

Jaws of a bench-vice clamp my temples.
My shoulders list under the weight
of a bag of slack.

My mouth belches exhaust fumes.
A concrete mixer masticates sludge
in my stomach. I shuffle

on feet glued to flagstones.
Skin tarred and feathered,
by the depression that steals

dopamine from my hacked brain.
A hammer smashes my breastbone,
exposing my prune heart.

I slither down muddy slopes,
daughter's skipping rope in one hand,
unopened blister pack of pills in the other.

Black Knight

My bed's mahogany legs stand on a Nepalese carpet.
I luxuriate in lying naked on silk sheets.
Brocade curtains fail to block car horns
and scraping heels on pavements.
Head lice scratch my scalp, debating today's events.
I close my eyes and the carpet flies.
It shakes as we encounter turbulence.
A black knight astride a grey mare lands
beside me, with a picnic basket of caviar and Champagne.
He says he still jostles and uses his lance.
I stoke the steel, say I miss him. We kiss.
Convulsions wake me. Aftershave lingers in the air.
The curtains waltz in the morning breeze.
How much longer will I meet him in my dreams?

How Did You Know?

For Hannah

'Mam, don't die on me while I'm gone.'
Your words octopus tentacles
that twist around my neural pathways.
Your father revs his van in the driveway.

I wave goodbye, shut the front door
slump to the hall floor. Octopus
releases its ink-black cloud,
blinds and chokes. Dark waters beckon.

I finger the note in my pocket,
dream of days I could swim with eels,
lounge on a lake's bed,
and gaze up at earth's ever-changing sky

no longer susceptible to its moods.
More of your words surface.
'Mam, my life would be screwed if you died.'
I haul myself to the bathroom

shower my body, cry myself dry,
watch fire flames curl my note.
How did you know
I loved you too much
to screw up your life again?

Death is Nothing At All

After Henry Scott-Holland

Death is not —
nothing.

It is everything.

It is not —
a negligible accident.

For my mother chose
to storm
into the next room.

Our laughter forgotten.

Now, I roam derelict buildings,
empty streets
screaming into the silent night.

Why couldn't God
have taken her
quietly?

Rodeo Cowboy on a Bronco

Grief grips my belly with his thighs,
grimaces as I stomp and snort,
inhales my excrement and his sweat,
roars as we burst from the chute.

He grazes the girth of my body with steel,
grips the leather rigging on my withers,
pulls his knees up as I buck,
then rolls his spurs along my shoulders.

Grief leans back as I descend
clings to me until I toss him to the ground.
He is the next cowboy who straddles me
just when I think I've broken free.

Saltwater Crocodile

Death is submerged
in a Northern Territory river,
she waits for earth to vibrate
from your hooves as you
and your herd come down
to the river's edge to drink.

Into the air, she leaps,
creates a waterfall out of calm water.
Her jaws clamp your hindquarters
and your friends flee.

She drags you underneath.
In the wake of your last breath,
she pulls you downriver to her burrow,
feasts on you for days.

Once sated, she will swim upriver,
submerge, wait until your herd forget
the dangers of murky waters
and they come to drink again.

Mr Sun

Two candles on your cake.
You search for Mr Sun with the *Teletubbies*.
Ask him to shine down on you,
sing with the Purple Dinosaur,
'I love you. You love me.
We're a happy family.'

Four candles on your cake.
You ram your red tractor against the kitchen door,
dig holes in the lawn with your JCB.
First earthquake hits – Magnitude 3.3.
We go on holidays to Granny and Grandad's,
leave Dad behind to save the turf.

Six candles on your cake.
You play in your bedroom with *Power Rangers*.
Your trucks become *Transformer* fighters.
Second earthquake hits – Magnitude 5.6.
We go on a longer holiday
to Granny and Grandad's.

Eight candles on your cake.
Head stuck in *Mario Brothers* on your PSP.
Your First Holy Communion – best day ever.
We buy a mountain bike out of your takings.
Dad misses your first cycle.
Third earthquake hits – Magnitude 7.7.

Ten candles on your cake.
You construct walls in *Minecraft*.
Dad leaves you home on a Sunday evening.
You run to the door, snuggle into my jumper.
His van roars down the driveway.

Twelve candles on your cake.
You refuse to blow them out, seek refuge
in the world you've built.

Google '*Is Santa real?*'
Scrawl Kill Me in your maths book.
I want to hug the sadness out of you.
We talk and talk the darkness away.

Fourteen candles on your cake.
You blow them out.
I agree not to *Facebook* the photo.
You play *Counterstrike* on your computer,
get a bench press for Christmas,
walk to the school gate, smiling.

My Therapist and Her Bumble Bee
For M

It circles overhead, like a drone,
as we revisit childhood wounds, talk of adult loss
and all that lurks in the space between.
The bee buzzes and burning Beech crackles

in the stove beside us. Smoke seeps through a chink
in the pipe, clouds the room, waters my eyes.
The buzz overpowers our words,
until the bee lands on a windowsill.

My therapist takes a tissue from a box,
approaches the insect. I'm afraid it will sting
her hand. She folds the tissue
around the fuzzy black and amber body

as if wrapping a gift, then lifts her parcel,
opens a window and releases the bee.
Its buzz fades and I'm jealous of its joy
in being free. Beech wood smoke

follows the bee into April air.
My therapist turns, with a smile that tells me,
this will be the last time
I see her pull a tissue from its box.

V

Excavation

I don't see a mountain
or white church resting on its peak
or grey shale sliding
towards the base
or the rocky stream
and channels it cuts
in its race towards the sea.
I don't see sheep clinging to its face
or barefoot pilgrims, stones
splashed with their blood.
I don't see wild purple heather
or trunks of trees
slanted by wind.

I see pick-axes loosening
centuries of clay
soil falling
revealing
grey-granite skin
a woman on her hunkers
heather becoming hair
cheek resting on knuckles
head lowered in prayer -
my Madonna.
Her eyes cast on the three hundred
and sixty-five islands spread
across the bay beneath.
I see the woman
I'm afraid to unearth
in case I lose her again.

Growth

I stride into the fog,
like scissors cutting through parchment.
Its low opacity allows
a forest to form.

I scrape moss that measles
a Pine's trunk, tear
at the dark bark:
it crumbles like shortcake.

I bore a hole through the rings
of many winters, thick resin oozes.
I watch it make its way
down the trunk like an overweight slug.

My heart empties and the spring sun
enters. I lie on the forest floor,
ear to ground, listen to the trees'
growing pains and remember my own.

Two for Joy
After Raymond Carver

My beloved stalks my mind
when I sit in my garden
and watch the birds. A screech
alerts me to a magpie perching
on my Weeping Birch.

I search the sky,
then scan the Blackthorn hedge
at the end of the garden,
hoping for a second bird.

Just as I'm about to stand
and race towards the black
and white winged-creature,
flapping my arms,
another lands beside her.
I sit back and listen
to them chattering.

Even though there are times
I've wished we'd never met,
I can't shoo my beloved away.
She gave me something
no-one else ever could.

Dim the Screens

Step into January air,
shield your eyes from winter sun,
listen to childish whispers,
or, perhaps, a distant cuckoo's song,

and the lowing of a pregnant cow.
Walk muddy paths by the Barrow
feel squelch of muck
engulf your synthetic soles.

Face into the frosty breeze,
stand at the water's edge
but keep your distance
from those stinging nettles.

Sit on the bench, acned with moss,
let it cushion your weary body,
cast your eyes over a flash
of white; a swan resting in the reeds.

Remember the maternal love
that once unearthed your voice,
then, like a sloth,
hang from the branch of an Alder

its canopy - the roof of your heart.
Eat and sleep there,
let new poems find first breath.

Fodder

I dig my pitchfork
into a wall of fermented grass,
harvested in May, for November.

Immune to its sulphurous gases,
I throw clumps into a feeding trough,
watch cattle lower their heads.

The wind is still for once,
and the only sound
is bovine chewing,
the swishing of mud-caked tails.

Nelly, too old for the mart
or butcher's knife,
stops mid-munch, raises her head.

Her brown eyes beckon me
to lay down my fork,
and give thanks
for surviving October.

Her breath, a cloud of translucent white,
rises towards a rare blue sky.
A breeze, not of this earth,
whispers.

Crossing the Threshold

At the end of winter-grey,
spring-yellow, summer-blue
and autumn-orange days

I close the front door,
go to my inner room
light a fire and sit

with a lover
who doesn't buy flowers
or chocolates or write Valentines.

I breathe in peat-smoke,
feel heat in my bones.
I exhale the greys, yellows, blues

and sit with a lover
who makes no sound,
has no form or scent.

In fact, I have no evidence
of a lover's existence.
I just sit

with a lover's unknowable vastness.

Joy

After Ballad (Joys of Life) oil on wood panel by Frantisek Kupka

Joy is a naked woman
sitting astride
a speckled-grey mare
raising her arms like

                a victorious marathon runner
                exposing the virgin-white
                of her underarms
                and *Babycham* breasts.

    Joy is her hands,
    bound by the untamed
    locks of her salted hair.
    I imagine mine
    delving into the folds
    of her unstarched body.

                Joy is another woman
                on a piebald, knees bent,
                her derriere, a reversed C,
                skin the colour
                of Uluru sandstone,
                lips parted.

Joy is the feel of hooves
sinking into damp sand,
oblivious to the tide
creeping towards them
like a white veil threatening
to shroud.

Joy is sitting
in Prague,
watching wild women ride.

You - the grey speckled mare
and I - the piebald pony.

Ariana's Scent

What I missed the most,
was your essence.
I never asked you what it was.
I searched shops, purchased

shower gels, shampoos, moisturisers,
body washes, perfumes,
so I could wear you on my skin.
I gave up looking in the end.

Yesterday, my daughter hopped
into the car,
'What's that smell?' I asked.
'It's Ariana Grande's new perfume.'

Last night, I crept into her room,
found what I was looking for,
brought Ariana Grande
to bed with me.

I Sat With Grief

She came after the children
were fed and put to bed
just when I thought
I had no tears left to cry.
She climbed into the bath
sat behind me.
I felt her in the fingers
that shampooed my hair,
in the loofah
that scoured dead cells
from my thighs.
The water grew cold
but she scalded my skin.
I watched red welts rise
and spread across my abdomen.

I heard her in the pop of the plug
when I yanked it upwards,
she gurgled in the water's swirl
down the drain.
I let her towel my body dry
and brush my hair.
She softened coarse strands
with coconut oil that smelt
of honeymoon nights.
I didn't rage, rationalise,
ignore or trivialise.
I just sat on the bath's lip
and cried, knowing
I would not be swept away.

I Kicked Open

my childhood home;
door hinges screeched.
I ducked when a house-wren
dropped from the rafters chirping
like an alarm clock. I yanked open cupboards,
swiped cobwebs, spiders fell. A whimper stopped
my foot from stamping the creatures, that once made
my six-year-old legs, leap into my mother's lap. The flagstones
parted. I crept downstairs. You were in the candle-lit cellar, alive,
waiting for me to set you free,

                              my wild and wonderful self.

A Christmas Blessing

May you quiver with Divine energies
and may you believe that in them
we live, and move, and have our being.

May you be aware of their presence
when you prepare your dinner
and when you sit and eat.

May you feel their breath on your cheek
when you close your eyes to sleep.
May you dance with them in your dreams.

May the Angel on your tree sing of their glory.
May their flame flicker in your heart
and their love gently prise you apart.

May you let go of all woes, and allow
Divine energies to heal, and live,
and move, in your being.

We'll Meet Again

in the liminal space of a spring tasting of tannin winter
but with the faint sweetness of a rose petal summer.
Light cobalt will colour the morning sky, the air
will be crisp as days when frost whitens country lanes.

March lambs will jump in the field beside your house.
We'll hear the trill of a blue tit perched on an Ash tree.
The year or two between that day and this
will dissolve with the memory of December's fog.

In the warmth of a minute's hug
we'll say goodbye to chats via screens.
I'll sit in your kitchen, sip tea and anticipate
the taste of the fruit cake baking in your oven.

January, 2021

I sit on a frosty bench beside the half-iced lake,
smile at a barking terrier and hooded stranger.

I whisper to robins hopping on the frozen ground,
notice for the first time their burnt-orange breasts.

Unknown Divine energies move through me.
My body trembles, hair electrifies, fingers tingle.

Unable to contain the Divine love within,
I unclench my fists. Heat rises from my palms.

I send it to you, in your hour of need.
My robins spread their wings and fly.

VI

Preparing for Death

Death is the new-born
who must leave the warmth
of her mother's body. It's the weaning baby
who must give up her sucking reflex, open her mouth,
allow spoons of tepid orange mush to land on her tongue.
It's the toddler, chubby legs upright for the first time, turning
her head, this way and that, looking at the world around her,
instead of gazing up at the sky. Myth would have us believe
that the elephant, anticipating death, walks to her own
burial ground. I used to think it was a saltwater crocodile
who leaped from calm waters and grabbed us, just when
we thought it was safe to drink. How can death pounce
unexpectantly when we spend our whole lives
walking towards it?

I look from my grandchild to mirror, trace
the lines that zig-zag across my forehead,
ask myself, 'Am I preparing for death?'
Will I slip back inside my mother's womb
or be pulled underwater by a crocodile?
We drape death around our shoulders,
like a thread-bare coat, making us
shiver in the depths of winter,
when all death really is -
is the arrival to our point
of departure, a stepping
onto another train.

Desecration of Time

Dali's clock slides
from the kitchen wall
onto the table.
Corona eats its face.
With nothing to hang
onto, Roman numerals
and steel hands slip
into the pond,
we call time,
strewn now with algae,
oil-slicked,
smelling of green diesel.
Days and dates drown.

My Menopausal Womb

The hairdresser empties tubes
into a black bowl, stirs a mixture
of what looks like day-old blood.
366, he calls the dye.

He pastes my greying hair,
it doesn't take long to cover.
Thirty minutes of flicking through *Image*,
Hello and *Good Housekeeping*
and I'm scarlet again.

The gynecologist puts my feet in steel stirrups
tells me to spread my legs
covers his hands with latex gloves
grabs a speculum
tells me to cough and inserts.

When he withdraws I know
what he has to say before he
opens his mouth. And I wish
there was a colour like *366*
that would turn my shrunken
womb scarlet again.

My Menopausal Vagina

is the village's oldest pub, doors wide open
she ignores medical experts who call closing time.
She doesn't miss sex hormones
that disappeared with dusk. She's still
quite the capable host, her parties never run dry.

She doesn't feel like a forgotten
World War 1 trench, full of sludge.
Prefers to think of herself as an estuary,
kayakers, windsurfers and paddlers
still want to explore. She delights
in their enjoyment of her brackish water,
that leaves a salty taste on the tongue.

My vagina is not a posy
that will welcome a man's nose.
She's ragweed, not easy to contain,
liable to poison mules and asses,
stupid enough to wander into her pasture
for a munch, ignoring the Women Only sign
she has erected at her entrance.

My Lioness
After Adrian Mitchell

When she was a cub,
she was happy
to play with my fingers.

I felt her twitch
at my first disco,
when I gaped at all the boys
and their little lions
tucked inside skinny jeans.

Clammy from dry ice,
she got wet when one
rubbed against her.

When I fell in love,
she opened wide, welcomed
a lion, clenched him until he filled
her with his milk.

Before long she was pushing
out babies and lost her muscle tone.

The gynaecologist stitched her up.
Lion preferred the back door.
She wasn't as wet as she used to be.

He lost his mane.
Wasn't as hard as he used to be.
Now she plays with a lion,
powered with batteries
and dreams of other lionesses.

Lioness or Labrador

Sometimes all I want,
is to be a lioness
pounce on my lover
tear at her clothes
as if pulling flesh
from the carcass of a fawn,
roar myself hoarse
while we wrestle
to be on top
and after, coated
in jungle sweat, lick my lips.

Sometimes all I want,
is to be a labrador
lie beside the stove
feel hands stroke my fur
watch lazily when a mouse sneaks
into the kitchen, stops
in the middle of the room,
looks at me watching him,
nibbles at a crumb
under the table
and waltzes out the patio door.

Talk To Me Like Lovers Do

I slip my legs into red silk knickers.
>Put on your control panel pants.

I clasp my transparent lace bra.
>Your breasts are going to sag in that rag.

I gaze into the tallboy mirror.
>Have you nothing better to look at?

I button up my new frost-blue blouse.
>That does nothing for your complexion.

I pull my faux leather skirt over my hips.
>You can't go shopping in that get-up.

I squeeze into my new turquoise shoes.
>No wonder you have bunions.

I spike my hair with some *L'Oréal* gel.
>What happened to your lovely permanent wave?

I lick seeds from passion fruit for breakfast.
>It's a bowl of porridge you should be eating.

I flick through the latest copy of *Diva* magazine.
>Since when did you stop reading *Good Housekeeping*?

I write a poem about having sex at sixty.
>You should be knitting scarfs for grandchildren.

Wrench

For Brian

I sip my tea, watch my son tie the laces
of his new steel-capped work boots,
slip his arms into a hi-vis vest
pick up his new toolbox
full of metal wrenches.

I stop myself from taking his photo
like I did when he pranced around
the kitchen trying to loosen
his new school tie.

When we arrive at the workshop,
I offer to go in with him.
'Mam!'
I watch him stride away,
notice for the first time,
he has the gait of a boy merging into man.

At the end of the day,
he smells of machine oil.
I eavesdrop on his conversation
with his dad who, he tells,
he needs a quarter-inch socket set.

I still hear the four-year-old
jabbering on about his new teacher,
and the sandpit in the school playground.
Bob The Builder hat on his head,
yellow plastic wrench in his hand.

VII
Voices
After Martina Evans

My Therapist's Dog
For Bailey

'Ah, jeez, not you again,' her golden retriever muttered,
as I stepped out of my car and slammed the door shut.

'When are you going to stop coming here?
She has to have two coffee pods
before your sessions. The doctor told her
to stop drinking. Sets her heart racing.
It's you - not the coffee.

What was going on at the last session?
I was having a grand sleep under the Elm tree
till you started giving out.
Fuck the crows
What have you got against crows?
They were highly insulted.

You've been coming here far too many years.
I said as much, to her last week.
She starts jabbering on about *transference,*
attachment and *detatchment.*
I had to go outside for a run, to clear my head.

Why do you have to hug her after every session?
She's your therapist, not your mother.'

'Stop snapping at my ankles,' I said,
as I tried to walk around her.

'Live with her for a few days,' she barked,
'If you saw her first thing in the morning,
or had to eat her burnt potato skins,
or sit at her feet and watch *Pointless* every night -
that'd knock the love out of you.

It's time for you to go live your own life,
get yourself a man or indeed a woman.

Stop wrecking our heads
with your *daddy never loved me stories*.
There's only so much of that,
a dog or a therapist can take.'

Ford Fiesta

She beeped her horn
when I tore the L plate from the back window.

'Keep the noise down,' I said,
'You'll wake the neighbours.'

'Took you long enough to pass the bloody test,
I lost count after seven.
Nothing's going to stop us now
from leaving this godforsaken hole
and that excuse for a husband of yours.'

'I didn't learn to drive just to leave him,'
I said.

She beeped her horn louder.
'You'll be dead by the time you're fifty
if you stay here. I'm not going to spend
the rest of my life
crawling up and down boreens,
dodging potholes and stray sheep
getting splatters of cow shite
all over my shiny fenders.

I want to let my engine loose,
do some donuts, burn some tar,
cruise on the motorway.

C'mon woman, live a little.
The last time I saw you smile
was on your wedding day.'

'That's not true,' I said.

'I'm talking about a real smile,' she said,
not the *Botox* one,
you've been sporting
for the last five years.'

Eel

I dove into the murky water, sank to the bottom
settled myself on the riverbed,
said *hello* to a passing eel.
He stopped, turned towards me
and poked me in the stomach.

'You don't belong here,' he said.

'I don't belong up there, either.'

'Every human that comes down here
whines about life having no meaning
and not knowing who they are anymore.
My head's wrecked from it all.'

'I jumped into the river,' I said,
'to get a bit of peace.
Everywhere I go, I hear voices.
The whole world's talking to me,
mice, dogs, surfboards.
Yesterday, it was an umbrella.'

'Christ, no wonder you're down here.
Humans talking to you
is bad enough without all that.
Well, all I wanted to say
was, scoot over a bit.
You're lying on my part of the bed.'

Moon

I lived in a musty tent for months.
I could crawl out of my sleeping bag,
and haul myself to standing,
but the heavy canvas clung to me all day.

I thought I would stay locked in the tent forever.
One night, as I lay in my sleeping bag,
eyes staring into darkness,
the moon hovered above and said,

'Let's find you a marque,
red with white stripes like the circus tent
you loved as a child, where your mother
bought you candy floss and
you laughed at the clowns until you cried.'

The roof of the tent singed
and a ray of light burst through.

'If you can't hope, I'll hope for you.'

I reached out, silver rays landed on my shoulders,
folded around me like a shrug.
They stayed there while I plodded
through the next day, and the next,
until all that remained of my black tent
was grey-white ash.

Dreamcatcher

I banged the snooze button on my alarm clock,
dragged myself out of bed and opened the window.
My dreamcatcher fluttered in the breeze and said,

'I'm sorry but I can't catch every nightmare you have.'

'Isn't that what you're supposed to do,' I muttered,
hunting for a clean pair of knickers.

'You had me working overtime last night,' she said.
'I'm not *Wonder Woman*.'

My tights laddered as I pulled them over my thighs.

'I wish I didn't have to go to work today.
Why am I feeling so shitty? I'm much better than I was last year.'

The breeze blew my dreamcatcher onto my pillow and she said,

'Just because you have me hanging over your bed
doesn't mean you won't get the odd nightmare.
Give yourself a break, take a duvet day.'

I lay down beside her and fell asleep again.

Umbrella

The hail pounded the pavement,
like nails hitting concrete.
I opened the wardrobe, grabbed my umbrella.

'I've missed you,' she said.

I shook her. Dust mites flew from her canopy,
landed on my nose and made me sneeze.

'I don't feel like talking today.'

'If you don't talk to me, who will you talk to?' she said.
'All the heads around here are too busy
looking at their phones to listen.
I'm a rare species.'

I had to admit, she was right.
She never told me to *pull myself together,*
or *cheer up - it might never happen.*
She'd hover over my head,
let me moan and groan,
and when the rain stopped,
she'd wait in the wardrobe
until it rained again.

Mouse

'Do you have any idea what a fabulous daughter you have?'
said the mouse, as I waded
through the mound of clothes on the bedroom floor.

'I don't know why you're always giving out to her
for leaving half-full mugs of hot chocolate
on her dressing table. I'm rather partial to a sip
of cold, hot chocolate. And we do have a fine feast
on the scraps of blueberry muffins.

Though we might be getting a bit plump
from all the sugar. I was only saying to the wife
the other day that she might have to go on a diet.

We get great entertainment watching her do her make-up.
Do you realise what a talented artist she is?
All you seem to do is give out about the dirty towels
and make-up pads she leaves in the bathroom.

Though, I could make your hair stand on end
if I told you about the hour-long conversations
she has Facetiming her pals. Ah no,
couldn't do that to her and you're better off
not knowing anyway.

But tell me, who's this Shane lad?
He seems to be popping up on her *Snapchat* a lot lately.
Sent her ten heart emojis yesterday.
And that wasn't lipstick that was on her neck
after the disco last Saturday night either.'

'I'm going to town to get a mouse trap later,' I said.

'Ah, you wouldn't want to do that to the poor buck's
willie. That'd break her heart.'

Laurel Hedge

'Look at the fumes coming out of that machine,'
said my Laurel hedge, as I mowed the lawn.
'Apart from what it's doing to the air,
it's destroying my lovely shiny leaves,
look how black they are.

Lawn mowers need to be serviced.
Isn't your son sick of telling you that?
He might be seventeen
but he has way more sense than you.
Who cuts their lawn in high heels?'

'They're old,' I said,
it doesn't matter if they get a few grass stains.'

'If I had arms,' the hedge said,
'I'd be raising them in disbelief.

When are you going to give me a trim?
Look at the state of me,
leaves sticking out in all directions,
branches gone wild.

If you paid the same attention to me
as you paid your hair, I'd be in great shape.
Why did you plant me
if you weren't going to look after me?

I saw the next-door neighbour
take a huge can of *Round-Up*
from the boot of her car yesterday,
I've a feeling she's going to be spraying
the bits of me hanging over her fence.
Fuck, that'll destroy me altogether.'

Surf Board

'Hey Babe,' he said, as I propped
him against my bedroom wall.

'I'm not a babe,' I said.

'Whatever you are, let's catch a wave,
It's been far too long.'

'Twenty-five years
and not a word out of you,' I said,
looking at my sow-skin thighs.

'There was no point in talking to you
when I was locked away in the attic.
Are ya gonna give me to your son?
He looks like a cool surfer dude.'

'God, no,' I said, laying him on my bed
and climbing on top
hoping he wouldn't notice
my no-longer flat tummy.

'I just want to remember
what it was like to catch
a wave in the Tasman Sea
without fear of cracking my arthritic knee.'

Vagina

'Don't you dare, write a poem about this conversation,'
said my vagina, as I toweled myself dry.

'You've enough written about sex, vulvas,
and unsatisfying penises. Get over it.
Write something different, use the Irish Sea,
Croagh Patrick or Clew Bay as your muse.
Everybody loves poems about landscapes.

I'm sick and tired of seeing my personal details
in print. Who wants to read about a menopausal
vagina or any other type?

You should be out looking for a man
instead of spending so much time writing.
Delving into the unconscious, you say.
Load. Of. Bull.
It's delving into me you should be doing.

That vibrator of yours is crying out to be used.
Though it's the real thing I want.
The buzz from that yoke gave me terrible headaches
the few times you used it.

That gay phase didn't work out very well either, did it?
Still, that doesn't mean you have to close up shop.
It's a bit of fresh air I need.
Can you not smell the must?
There's mould starting to grow down here.'

Red Admiral

I was pulling weeds in the rockery,
when she alighted on my shoulder and said,

'I don't care what anyone else says,
You're A   W   E   S   O   M   E'

I let the dandelion in my hand
fall to the ground, reached toward my shoulder.
Her wings fluttered against my palms.

'Be careful or you'll squash me.
I'm only after escaping from my pupa
it's much too soon for me to die,
we still have a lot of living to do.'

Cygnet

After Emily Dickinson

Listen to your cygnet whisper,
'Enough is enough.'
Grasp Emily's *hope with feathers*.

Wade through the wooded swamp,
knee-deep in dank muck,
grab a Downy Birch branch and rise.

Cut the curly-leaved waterweed,
that litters your cyan lake
threatening to pull you under.

Skitter along the lake's surface,
until you have enough speed
to lift your feet. Then soar.

About the Author

Anne Walsh Donnelly lives in the west of Ireland. She writes poetry, prose and plays. She describes her writing process as 'Bungee jumping, naked, off the Cliffs of Moher.' Her poetry is wild and wonderful, honest and brave.

She was shortlisted for the Hennessy/Irish Times New Irish Writing Award in 2019 and selected for the Poetry Ireland Introduction Series in the same year. She was awarded a Words Ireland Mentorship in 2020 and a bursary from the Dublin Gay Theatre Festival.

She is the author of the poetry chapbook, *"The Woman With An Owl Tattoo"* (Fly On The Wall Poetry Press, 2019), which is a reflection on her growth since the ending of her marriage, an exploration of her sexuality and coming out in mid-life. The collection was awarded second prize in the International Poetry Book Awards in 2020. She is also the author of the short story collection, *"Demise of the Undertaker's Wife"* (Blue Nib, 2019).

Anne travels purposely in life towards an as-yet-unknown destination.

About Fly on the Wall Press

A publisher with a conscience.
Publishing high quality anthologies on pressing issues, chapbooks and poetry
products, from exceptional poets around the globe.
Founded in 2018 by founding editor, Isabelle Kenyon.

Other publications:

Please Hear What I'm Not Saying
Persona Non Grata
Bad Mommy / Stay Mommy by Elisabeth Horan
The Woman With An Owl Tattoo by Anne Walsh Donnelly
the sea refuses no river by Bethany Rivers
White Light White Peak by Simon Corble
Second Life by Karl Tearney
The Dogs of Humanity by Colin Dardis
Small Press Publishing: The Dos and Don'ts by Isabelle Kenyon
Alcoholic Betty by Elisabeth Horan
Awakening by Sam Love
Grenade Genie by Tom McColl
House of Weeds by Amy Kean and Jack Wallington
No Home In This World by Kevin Crowe
The Goddess of Macau by Graeme Hall
The Prettyboys of Gangster Town by Martin Grey
The Sound of the Earth Singing to Herself by Ricky Ray
Inherent by Lucia Orellana Damacela
Medusa Retold by Sarah Wallis
Pigskin by David Hartley
We Are All Somebody
Aftereffects by Jiye Lee

Social Media:
@fly_press (Twitter)
@flyonthewall_poetry (Instagram)
@flyonthewallpress (Facebook)
www.flyonthewallpress.co.uk

Praise for Anne Walsh Donnelly's debut chapbook:
The Woman With an Owl Tattoo

"*The Woman With an Owl Tattoo* is a poetry collection I recommend to those who marvel at a clear night sky full of stars, or those who pause and admire an enormous oak tree. I recommend it to those who revel in earthly comforts and embrace their desires. The poems feel as though they have been rough-hewn out of Donnelly's psyche. Alternating between cheeky, romantic, sensual, and moody, the poems bring fresh joy to ordinary moments and an understated Irish warmth to the genre."
- Gertrude Press

"It is an emerging of a woman from the chrysalis of heteronormative culture into a woman who reels and relishes the female form, casts off her obligations and embraces life."
- Rachel Reads It

"The honesty of this book is powerful, masterly in the way it is presented, and this makes for a book that makes an impression."
-The Northern Reader

"Raw, honest poetry at its finest. These poems are brave and I highly respect Donnelly for sharing such personal thoughts and feelings with her readers. A strong woman who is an inspiration to us all to be true to ourselves, no matter what age you are."
- Bunny's Pause